MYSTE

in the
CORNISH LANDSCAPE

Tamsin Thomas

BOSSINEY BOOKS

ACKNOWLEDGEMENTS
Front cover photography: RAY BISHOP
Other photographs: RAY BISHOP; JAMES LYNE; WOOLF-GREENHAM
Drawings: FELICITY YOUNG
Maps – Pages 94, 95: FELICITY YOUNG

First published in 1991 by Bossiney Books, St Teath, Bodmin, Cornwall.
Typeset and printed by Penwell Print Ltd, Callington, Cornwall.

ISBN 0 948158 67 0

ABOUT THE AUTHOR
- and the book

T*AMSIN THOMAS* lives in the beautiful south Cornwall port of Fowey with her husband Paul and dog, Dodger, just across the river from Polruan where she grew up. Her name suggests a Cornish background and indeed her father's family originates from The Lizard. She has married a Welshman, bringing together two great Celtic nations. Tamsin was educated at Fowey Comprehensive and St. Austell Sixth Form College before studying under the late Colonel 'Bill' Froud to become a riding instructor. She then trained as a radio journalist and started her career with the BBC in 1983 as a reporter with BBC Radio Cornwall when the Truro-based station first went on air.

She has recently returned to the station as a producer having spent two years as press officer with the National Trust in Cornwall. Tamsin's hobbies include rowing in Fowey's pilot gig, walking with her spaniel, Dodger, and taking trips with her father Mike in his open fishing boat 'Heritage'.

Tamsin Thomas is a traveller *par excellence.* Like the great Lady Clara Vyvyan of Trelowarren, she has an adventurous spirit. She can make a visit to the Men-an-Tol a real adventure. As befits a skilful broadcaster, she has a natural curiosity about people and places.

In this, her debut for Bossiney, Tamsin makes a fascinating tour among the *Mysteries in the Cornish Landscape.* She takes us to locations as different as Chun Castle down in Penwith and The Hurlers on the eastern edge of Bodmin Moor. She visits the strange carvings in Rocky Valley and speculates about the Once and Future King at King Arthur's Hall. Such is her enthusiasm and communica-

STONE CIRCLES ... An essential part of the mystery and magic of the Cornish landscape.

tion we travel with her. As do photographer Ray Bishop and illustrator Felicity Young.

'This,' says publisher Michael Williams, 'is a book that has needed doing for a long time, featuring as many as 30 mysterious locations in Cornwall. It's a Bossiney book for everyone and Tamsin's writing is as lively and refreshing as her BBC Radio Cornwall broadcasts.'

CORNISH MYSTERIES

I HAVE always enjoyed a vivid imagination.

As a child my self-induced day dreams about white horses and far-away islands landed me in a good deal of trouble. Today I am thankful for the ability to make books, music and places come alive inside my head providing a private world of excitement in which I can travel. My rambles through Cornwall are always filled with magic. Sometimes that magic comes from marvelling at the beauty which surrounds me, especially on the cliffs near Polruan where the National Trust take a caring role, and where I have walked for many years. Sometimes it originates from a strange intrusion on my expected view: a weathered slice of timber on the beach, a stranger on the footpath, a standing stone in the field.

C.E. Vulliamy, writing in his book *Unknown Cornwall* seventy years ago talked of 'word associations' – an exercise which requires you to react with a word or statement immediately another person says something to you. He said that if he were asked to react instantly to the word Cornwall he would 'without hesitation' say 'moors'. While understanding his reaction, I would have to say my answer would steer more towards 'ancient landscape' – a term I devised having been asked 'How would you best describe Cornwall?'.

In Cornwall you are in touch with ancient things.

Even today as the 20th century draws to its close, certain parts of Cornwall remain cloaked in mystery.

'Grey recumbent tombs of the dead in desert places
Standing stones on the vacant wine-red moor,

Hills of sheep, and homes of the silent vanished races
And winds, austere, and pure . . .'

Robert Louis Stevenson may not have been writing specifically of Cornwall, but the cleansing breezes of his poetry still flow over the mysterious and often secret landscapes of Cornwall. A cluster of grey fallen stone, a broken forgotten wall; men and women lived, worked and died in this westerly land yet left little or no recorded history. But such ruins are as much part of our Cornish heritage as, say, Truro Cathedral or our chapels inspired by John Wesley – or great houses like Lanhydrock on the edge of Bodmin Moor or Trelowarren down on The Lizard.

Before we begin our journey – pilgrimage, really – a few words of caution. *Mysteries in the Cornish Landscape* is not a guide book to the archaeological sites of Cornwall. It does not pretend to be a comprehensive catalogue of all the mysteries in the Cornish landscape. That would require a book of a thousand pages. I am merely an interested observer keen to explore the ancient times of which we know so little, letting my imagination fill in the gaps.

Many of my journeys began by looking at a map, for the best of Cornwall is now to be found on foot or horseback. It is largely in search of this Cornwall that I have travelled. The one-inch Ordnance Survey map is really a must on this kind of exploration.

No Cornish lane or track is quite as short or for that matter, anywhere near as long as that old character leaning over a gate told you half-an-hour ago – or was it an hour?

What is a mystery?

I turned to *Collins English Dictionary* and found:

'. . . *an unexplained or inexplicable event, phenomenon etc; a person or thing that arouses curiosity or suspense because of an unknown, obscure or enigmatic quality* . . .' There were other definitions, but I was happy to settle for these and believe my Cornish mysteries come within that range.

Charles Dickens said he had known no parallel in his memory to the experience of seeing the sun set over the Atlantic from Land's End.

Despite development and the growth of tourism, Cornwall still

SUNSET ... Day draws to a close at Land's End. The sight of the sun setting over the Atlantic from Cornwall's famed peninsula was for ever enshrined in the memory of the novelist Charles Dickens.

manages to generate unique experience. But usually you will need to get off the beaten track.

The late Ruth Manning-Sanders who lived near Land's End for many years touched on this unique quality in her fine book *The West of England:*

'The sea is almost everywhere in sight, and always within hearing. In times of tempest its long roar fills earth and sky; in times of calm the light winds carry its throb and rumble over fields and moors as if some giant were at work, thrashing corn. The whole district is thick with folklore; the flat boulders on the moors are giants' bob-buttons, the logan rocks their quoits, the hill forts their castles, the water-worn hollows in the stones their bowls and cups, the long flat rocks their beds and tables, and the massive lumps of granite that strew the hillsides bear witness to their ferocious battles. Trebiggan, Bolster, Wrath, Holiburn, Blunderbus – their names survive; their huge shapes, received back into the earth that made them, sleep, turned to stone, among the hills and cliffs.

When you get out on to the Cornish moors, you find yourself in touch with a prehistoric man. The circles and the huts, the ancient fortresses and the quoits – you find yourself in the past as well as the present – that, at least, is my experience.

Time in some curious way suffers a contraction – the here and now and the long ago seem oddly near to each other. You sense you are close to those old people, the ancient builders. The writer C.E. Vulliamy on a visit to Cornwall back in the 1920s, researching his book *Unknown Cornwall* said: *'I have seen vaster ruins in wilder places, but I have never felt the same intimacy with the primitive and prehistoric ...'*

Seventy years on, the remoter parts of Cornwall remain a mysterious land. As a passionate believer in the protection of Cornwall's countryside, I hope that in seventy years future 'explorers' will be able to stride forward, filled with the same excited curiosity as mine. May they too enjoy these ancient Celtic sites which link us to a world lost in the Cornish mists of time.

THE PAST ... Prehistoric man has left his mark on the Cornish landscape – and modern man still wonders at the ancient monuments he built.

Felicity Young

I am fortunate that the great majority of the present day photographs have been taken by Ray Bishop of Wadebridge, a man who has been photographing the Cornish landscape for more than forty years. Many of these photographs have been especially commissioned for this publication. There are some fine drawings too by Felicity Young of Tintagel who, like Ray, understands the subtleties of the terrain of Cornwall. Felicity has a special feel for the native stones. This then is an exploration in words and pictures – come, let us begin our *Mysteries in the Cornish Landscape.*

SEA AND SKY ... The seas that surge around our coastline and the cliffs that tower above peaceful coves are as much a part of our Cornish landscape as the moors and inland valleys. Indeed, perhaps you cannot really begin to understand the real Cornwall without taking in scenes such as this – Kennack Sands on The Lizard Peninsula.

CHUN CASTLE

AS I STOOD on the once majestic wall of Chun Castle, the ancient Penwith landscape stretched out before me on all sides, its wild rugged beauty surrounding the fort like a peaceful cloak. A magnificent example of an Iron Age hillfort, Chun was built entirely of stone, and today enough remains to give the visitor like myself a good idea of how it would have looked when in use. I freely admit to being a professional day-dreamer and standing at the entrance to Chun with the Celtic kingdom of Penwith at my feet I could hear the cries of warriors, feel the clash of weapons and smell the rancid odour of fear.

Chun Castle lies on the edge of the famous Tinners Way, or Old St Ives Road, which runs from the St Just area to Mounts Bay. For the lazy visitor investigating Penwith by car, it is signposted off the Penzance-Morvah road at Bosullow Common. Far better, I think, to discover Chun Castle by following in the steps of the miners and merchants whose tin and copper industry it once protected.

Chun, an abbreviation of Chy-an-woon or house on the downs, is made up of two huge concentric walls, the outer one of which still manages to afford some protection for the fort's interior, though it is now much reduced in height. You can still pass through the original entrance where Chun's massive gateposts stand guard. Tactics are always a vital part of defence and it is interesting to note that at one stage in Chun's varied career, the inner entrance, which was roughly in line with the outer one, was moved to create a staggered path. The theory behind this modification was that if intruders made it through the first entrance they would have to expose their right

THE SCENE BELOW ... Looking back towards Mount's Bay on the path to Chun Castle.

sides to the enemy on the inner wall while making for the second 'gateway'.

An ancient well still exists inside the fort and is said never to dry up even in the hottest of summers, but, sadly, it has now been filled with stones and rubble. The foundations of Dark Age buildings and a smelting furnace have also been discovered within the fort, fascinating pieces of the complicated jigsaw which, put together, gives some idea of the fort's long and diverse history.

Pottery has also been found, the most interesting piece being typical of work manufactured in the eastern Mediterranean before Caesar's time and until after the Roman era. If only these artefacts could talk, what tales they might tell of long, adventurous journeys, of foreign lands and people long since forgotten.

The castle has stood up well to the test of time, but its ravaged and ruinous look is not entirely due to the elements. In the last century it became a useful source for stone for the construction of property. I am pleased that the building trade did not strip Chun entirely of its character, and I hope it will remain a magical place to visit for many years to come.

CHUN QUOIT

JUST 300 yards away from Chun Castle is the excellently preserved Neolithic tomb, Chun Quoit. A classic example of the simple closed box chamber, it is formed by four large slabs supporting a capstone. It is the only Quoit in West Penwith with its capstone still in position and given its proximity to the Castle, it is quite remarkable that it was not pillaged for stone at the time the fort was being constructed.

The Quoit represents a huge feat of engineering and is one of those bold, yet simple, structures which has a rugged beauty of its own. I chose not to venture inside, access is anyway very difficult, but in 1871 W.C. Borlase found it had a shallow internal pit which had long since been rifled. He suggested that as a result of this the interior is probably deeper than it had been originally.

Just who might be buried beneath the Quoit is a secret known only to Mother Earth, but the original occupant must surely represent a mighty and advanced race. How many of our buildings will stand for thousands of years I wonder?

MEGALITHIC TOMB … Great prehistoric tombs such as Chun Quoit still hold mysteries for us today. Legends survive of magical healing powers coming from the massive stones of such structures. Chun Quoit has just one chamber and is set in a round barrow about 35ft across.

MEN-SCRYFA

IF ONLY we could travel into the past and witness great moments from Cornwall's history. I would choose to visit West Penwith in the 6th century AD when Cornish royalty fought great battles and the wild landscape played silent witness to a lifestyle long since lost in the misty clouds of time.

The Men-Scryfa or Stone of Writing, stands alone like a granite sentinel guarding the countryside, in a field 325 yards past the Men-an-Tol. This for me is a truly exciting stone as on its northern face is a clue to its history; an inscription to the memory of RIALOBRAN – CVNOVAL – FIL – (Rialobran, Son of Cornwall.)

An ancient story suggests that Rialobran was killed at the Battle of Gendhal Moor defending his father's territory after it had been seized by an invader. The royal family had been forced to flee the land, but Rialobran chose to face the foe on the moors where the Men-Scryfa stands. It is said that he was buried by the stone after being slain and experts claim that the existence of the monument suggests the battle was won, meaning the brave warrior did not die in vain.

Legend has it that the Prince was buried with all his arms and treasures – an interesting thought but unfortunately one that led to the stone falling down in the early 19th century. Apparently a local man, who hankered for riches, heard that gold had been found beneath the great stone and, crazed by greed, dug a deep pit round the Men-Scryfa which eventually undermined it and brought it down. Fortunately it was re-erected by the Antiquarian Society in 1862, though it was sunk deeper than it had originally been.

Treasure hunters can ruin the landscape. Happily Cornwall has a knack of holding on to her hidden secrets, just sometimes revealing them when they are least expected.

'This part of Penwith,' said fellow Bossiney author Sally Jones in her *Legends of Cornwall*, 'is so heavy with history and legend that at times the farms and cottages of today seemed dwarfed by their backcloth – a landscape where in times past mighty dreams, human and supernatural, were played out, whose echoes and traces now remain "stamped on these lifeless things".'

MEN-AN-TOL

THE MEN-AN-TOL fires the imagination, immediately posing a host of delicious unanswered questions: who fashioned the crude hole in the rugged granite? Why were the stones erected in the first place? Does the monument hold mysterious healing powers? Such questions and years of speculation have ensured that this holed stone and many others like it in the British Isles, have kept their fascination.

The name Men-an-Tol comes from the Cornish Mên or Maen meaning Stone, and Tol meaning Hole, though it is also known as the Crick Stone, crick being a spasm or cramp. This second name probably relates to the healing powers the Men-an-Tol is said to hold for children and adults alike.

For youngsters with rickets or other such diseases, the healing process involves them being dragged through the hole in the centre stone 'nine times against the sun'; adults have to crawl round the stone before climbing through if they want to rid themselves of lumbago or sciatica.

It may all sound like a well rehearsed legend skilfully crafted to attract the inquisitive tourist, but people do still travel to the Men-an-Tol with poorly children. When publisher Michael Williams and I visited the site we were both feeling fit and well and so could not test the stone's power. In fact it took us two attempts to reach this strangely peaceful monument which is signposted off the Morvah road and lies at the end of a well-trodden path. Our first visit was cut short by a stinking lake of mud and manure on a day when we had both forgotten our wellingtons! We turned back disappointed,

SPECULATION ... Publisher Michael Williams and author Tamsin Thomas ponder the mysteries of Men-an-Tol. Although the stones are away from the main road, experts are becoming worried by the number of visitors to the historic site, their feet literally undermining the 10,000 year old structure. A site protection scheme was put underway in 1990.

but on reflection the quag was a fortunate discovery as I set out on our second visit better equipped for a walk on the moor and with an eager anticipation for a treasure denied me first time round.

There are those who strive to seek a scientific or historical reason for the Men-an-Tol's existence and the alignment of the stones. I for one prefer to speculate on its past and imagine the people and traditions it was first associated with.

LANYON QUOIT

LEGEND says that King Arthur dined at this site, which lies 2½ miles north of Madron, on the eve of his final battle. At the gathering Merlin predicted that Arthur and his chieftains would gather here again just before the end of the world. It would be interesting to witness that reunion and hear the comments from those privileged to have seen the area at each end of a huge, and some would say destructive, expanse of time.

Lanyon Quoit is one of the largest and most perfect examples of its kind still in existence, and is all that remains of a megalithic chambered long barrow. The huge 13½ ton capstone is supported by three pillars, the overall shape resembling a primitive table, hence its other name – The Giant's Table.

Sadly, the Quoit is not standing in its original form. Around the time of the Battle of Waterloo it fell. Some say it came down during a violent storm, others claim it was undermined by constant digging around its base which disturbed the pillars. Whatever the reason, it is unfortunate because the Quoit must originally have been a breathtaking site as it stood high enough for a rider on horseback to pass underneath.

Lanyon Quoit was given to the National Trust in 1952 by Lt-Col, later Sir, Edward Bolitho, and is now guaranteed a safe passage through time.

WHERE ARTHUR DINED … Or so the legend goes. Lanyon Quoit was reconstructed in 1824. Before its collapse it stood much higher, serving as a symbol of territorial ownership as well as a burial place for clan leader or king.

MORE MODERN AT MADRON

I HOPE you will forgive me if I wander slightly from the trail of the mysterious to indulge in a more modern theme. Refreshment is a vital tonic to the traveller and I, in discovering these ancient corners of Cornwall, have crossed the threshold of a hostelry or two. This one at Madron in West Cornwall, is clearly a little older than me! But its lichen-strewn thatch and weathered stone facade radiate a Cornish character seen rarely in these days of tiled roofs and pebble-dashed walls.

I cannot help wondering what led to the position of the men in this 1870 photograph, so rurally resplendent in their 'out-of-place' top hats and watch-chain-clad waistcoats. Are they chatting awkwardly to each other as the photographer, a stranger perhaps, fusses and fiddles to capture the scene? Have they fallen out and chosen to stand well apart without losing the opportunity to appear? Whatever the reason, they and the woman sheltering shyly in the doorway, create a glimpse into a past world.

When I first saw this picture my eye was drawn to the far left hand side where a woman, a neighbour perhaps, is watching the activity from her window, ignorant maybe of the fact that she has become a subject. That is one part of village life that has survived the test of time – just watch the curtains flicker next time you raise your camera in the street!

A CORNISH INN ... Landlord John Michell served 'beer, porter and spirits' according to the notice over the door. It seems likely that his usual customers were roughly-dressed working men rather than the splendidly-garbed trio in the photograph.

JOURNEY TO THE STONES … The circle that waits to be discovered by the determined and, below, *windswept trees on the secret road to Boscawen.*

BOSCAWEN-ÛN STONE CIRCLE

IT WAS so exciting to 'discover' Boscawen-ûn stone circle, the almost secret circle which is reached by following a rough farm track outside the village of St Buryan. Exciting because these stones are not easily accessible, or visible from the road, like many others in Cornwall. On my first visit I had almost convinced myself that I had taken the wrong track as I wandered past trees warped and twisted by the harsh West Cornwall winds, when suddenly there they were, nineteen stones in the morning sun standing around a huge granite pillar which leaned dramatically towards the north-east. This phallic middle stone is said to represent masculinity, while another in the circle made from a large block of white quartz, portrays femininity. Both make this unique among the circles of Penwith.

I found myself drawn to the middle stone – when I touched it it appeared to be giving off a comforting warmth, probably created by the morning sun shining on it. I know there are many sceptics who ridicule those who believe the stones have special powers or meanings, but does it not make sense for a woman to be attracted to that which represents masculinity?

Ian Cooke in his book *Journey To The Stones* thus describes a visit to the circle just after the summer solstice in 1986 when he arrived shortly before dawn:

'As the sun rose, I could see two very sharp and most unnatural shadows low down on the northern face of this pillar. On closer examination they turned out to have been caused by the sides of two elongated triangular 'axe-heads' which had been cut into the stone. They were obviously very ancient

and had been weathered so that the edges and corners were rounded. Once the sun rose higher and moved over to the right this face of the pillar was left in shadow, and the axes 'melted' into the surrounding granite – no wonder I had never noticed them before.'

Mr Cooke explains the axes were used to clear undergrowth ready for crop planting and so had strong connotations of fertility and renewal through destruction.

Craig Weatherhill who is a Bard of the Gorsedd of Cornwall, says the monument is probably the Beisgawen yn Dumnonia named in the old Welsh Triads as one of the 'Three Principal Gorsedds' of the Island of Britain. The modern Cornish Gorsedd first met here in 1928.

During the centuries some of the stones have fallen. Three were re-erected in 1862 when a hedge which cut across the circle was also removed – unfortunately the stones have not always been put back in their original positions.

For me this is one of the highlights of any visit to West Penwith. The circle has a serene, welcoming atmosphere while still challenging the modern world to dare encroach on its wonderfully unspoilt surroundings. Long may it remain an 'almost secret' circle.

SYMBOL OF MASCULINITY ... The central pillar of the stone circle rears dramatically upwards in the morning sun.

MERRY MAIDENS

THE POPULAR story surrounding this well known and carefully preserved stone circle, does tie in with the forces of energy that some believe the stones are charged with. According to the legend, one Sunday evening when the god-fearing folk around Lamorna and St Buryan were at prayer, a boisterous group of young girls defied the call of the church and strayed into the fields. Here two evil spirits, disguised as pipers, enticed them to dance by playing lively tunes. The rhythm got faster, the dancing more furious, but as the proceedings reached a crescendo a bolt of lightning transfixed the whirling revellers. The nineteen stones are said to be the maidens, frozen forever for their sins – the two tall stones nearby, the wicked pipers. The pent-up energy in the stones could be enormous, given that they were young girls paralysed at the height of their carefree festivities.

The stones, which date back to the Bronze Age, form a true circle with just one gap, on the eastern arc. This could well have been an entrance, or it may just be the site of a further stone which has succumbed to the rigours of time. Three of the stones are known to have fallen in the past as they were re-erected during a restoration project at the circle in the 1860s.

Historically it is possible that this exposed field with its striking view over the hauntingly unchanged Penwith landscape, was the site of the last great battle in the west when the Saxons, led by King Aethelstan, defeated King Howel and the Cornish army. In this context, the pipers and the circle are more likely to represent the rival kings surrounded by the bodies of those slain in battle.

I visited the Merry Maidens on an early winter's morning when the dew still sparkled on the grass and weak sun filtered through the calm air. I was struck by the beauty of the circle and the peace which surrounded it. The cattle grazed nonchalantly, seemingly unimpressed by this mystical monument, but I felt a strange warmth, too strong to have come from the winter sun, but strong enough to warrant explanation; perhaps there is an energy exuding from the stones?

I leave the Merry Maidens with a passage from Peter Underwood's book, *Mysterious Places: 'The Merry Maidens leave different impressions on different people. To me they are the silent witnesses of a past way of life with a meaning that we have yet to discover and they contain a power of some kind that is almost pulsating in its intensity; they are truly fascinating'.*

CLOSE-UP … A section of the circle showing the carefully-trimmed stones and well-preserved stones. Here, they look their best in the sparkling winter sunshine.

COVES OF CONTRAST

HAVING travelled often to The Lizard, from where my father's family originates, I am of the opinion that the whole of the peninsula is a mystery. It exudes a protective air, suggesting to the stranger that it will not reveal its secrets lightly; and there are many to be discovered if you care to take the time and the interest.

This is a peninsula of contrasts. Wild heathlands, home to rare clovers and heathers, spread daringly towards the often angry seas, overhead, helicopters buzz like military bees, on exercise from the nearby Culdrose Naval Air Station.

Sheltered havens, naturally created in the sea-battered rock, fire a wealth of images: windblown and salt-caked sailors struggling from the wild water's edge, victims of a shipwreck; stealthy dark-clothed smugglers creeping silently up steep paths laden with brandy and tobacco. Today you are more likely to witness brightly coloured cars, inquisitive families and corduroy clad walkers – a penalty of Cornwall's beauty? A question you must answer yourself.

Gunwalloe Church Cove is not only one of the loveliest on the peninsula but in the whole of Cornwall. If there's a strong south westerly blowing, a furious sea pounds on to these rocks. This cove is steeped in shipwreck and legend. Folklore says the attractively simple church, nestling on the shore, was built by sailors who survived the terrors of the sea. In reality an early church was constructed to serve nearby residents, and today the present building, erected in the fourteenth and fifteenth centuries, is a Cornish curiosity with its eye-catching tower strangely detached from the church. Services are held regularly at Gunwalloe – conducted by the Vicar

LITTLE CHANGED ... An old postcard of Gunwalloe Cove and Church.

of Cury.

Between Gunwalloe Church Cove and Gunwalloe Fishing Cove, you'll find Dollar Cove. This stretch of coastline has witnessed many tragedies, for the fickle face of The Lizard can change abruptly with the arrival of stormy weather.

The King of Portugal's treasure ship fell victim to the evil clutches of a Cornish storm in 1527, and in the eighteenth century a Spanish ship was wrecked nearby taking with it a secret which has truly become a mystery to treasure seekers. Rumour has it that she carried a cargo of Silver Dollars, a tale which still lures the inquisitive, and has led to the area being known locally as 'Dollar Cove'. Is there a fistful of treasure lying in wait below the shifting sands and anxious waters? If there is, I hope it is never found as it might shatter the mystery which infuses the Cove and the visitor.

DOLLAR COVE ... Do Spanish silver dollars lie hidden beneath the churning seas off Dollar Cove? Local people are still convinced that treasure trove is there to be found – by someone, someday.

INTREPID SEEKERS ... Right, *publisher Michael Williams clutches the map, author Tamsin Thomas looks warily back while ahead their canine companion waits impatiently – who knows what is around the next corner of a Cornish lane?*

ROSEMERRYN FOGOU

I WAS reluctant to enter the fogou at first, unsure about crossing the low stone-beamed threshold, and yet I felt strangely drawn towards the granite entrance and narrow passageway beyond. Once inside, fear drained from me like an ebbing tide, giving way to a peaceful warmth that provided instant reassurance.

Fogous are a mystery, both to the amateur and professional historian who have guessed at their purpose but never found a definite answer. These strange underground structures with long passages clad in roughly hewed granite stones, have consistently defied the attentions of researchers, and left historians and scholars baffled. Archaeologists suggest they could have provided storage, shelter or some form of defence, and the possibility that they were used for religious ceremonies has not been totally ruled out.

The word 'fogou' comes from an old Celtic word once used to describe both natural and man-made caves, but these are not to be confused with the element-eroded hollows found in soft rock, often at the water's edge. Probably built in the early Iron Age, the obvious care given to their construction suggests the fogous were socially important.

Rosemerryn fogou stands near the Lamorna River not far from St Buryan, and is a superb example of these mysterious granite galleries. Its religious atmosphere is heightened by the presence of a carving depicting a healing entity or spirit, and the curved bank at the north-eastern end emphasises the feminine qualities sometimes given to such constructions. It is believed that these less formal parts of the fogou represented birth and caring, the curve

reflecting the womb.

Visitors have apparently reacted in various ways when visiting Rosemerryn: some have felt ill while others have experienced vivid imagery. I simply discovered the peace, and enjoyed a calming warmth such as that experienced when you sit in a sun-drenched window on a winter's day and let the rays gently play on your back. Whatever its purpose all those hundreds of years ago, Rosemerryn now provides an exciting and fascinating link with the past that is remarkably intact.

LINK WITH THE PAST … We can only guess at the purpose of this man-made granite cave.

WESLEY'S STONE

THE TINY village of Zennor snuggles in a sheltered hollow between the sea and the Penwith moors. It is a settlement which has bravely survived a lifetime trapped between two powerful elements; the fickle Atlantic Ocean that can one day rage and another day caress and the moorland wind which can whisper or roar depending on its mood.

The land around Zennor has been farmed over thousands of years and now holds the secrets of generations. It is no doubt the age of this ancient landscape that has led to the legends and tales that even now surround it.

As you enter Zennor from the Lands End side you pass a large boulder of granite which lies on the grass verge. From this bold stone you can enjoy a view down over Zennor and away towards the church, a view which many a weary traveller must have marvelled at after a blustery hike across the moors.

Given its vantage point above the village, it is easy to understand why the Methodist preacher, John Wesley chose the stone as a natural pulpit from which to spread the word of the Lord.

Today the preacher's granite stage stands as a memorial stone to the man whose sermons changed many a Cornishman's life.

Wesley hit Cornwall and the Cornish like a gale blowing in off the Atlantic, shattering old ideas and values, waking many of the Anglican parsons from their comfortable slumber and making some sort of sense to life for ordinary working people. He may have needed to stand on this stone to make himself heard, but he spoke a language the people understood. It was Wesley who prodded the

THE VILLAGE BELOW ... Opposite, *Looking down over Zennor from the Wesley Stone.*

MAN OF THE PEOPLE ... *John Wesley, whose remarkable preaching brought great changes to the people of Cornwall.*

Cornish conscience on the subject of smuggling and wrecking. 'A smuggler then, and in proportion, every seller or buyer of uncustomed goods is a thief of the first order, a highwayman, or a pick-pocket of the worst sort.'

Wesley's physical achievements alone were enormous. He rode over 250,000 miles, sometimes covering seventy miles and delivering three sermons in the same day. He preached more than 45,000 sermons – not a few of them before hostile assemblies, even here in Cornwall he had to cope with an occasional riot. He wrote 233 original works, including a four volume History of England, earning in the process £40,000 and giving every penny of it away. In addition to all this, he set up a free medical dispensary, adapted an electrical machine for healing, opened spinning and knitting shops for the poor, and founded the Kingswood School for boys at Bristol, writing the text books himself.

THE LOGAN STONE

MAN'S DESIRE to meddle has affected many aspects of our country and its natural wonders, so it didn't surprise me to find that the massive rocking Logan Stone once fell victim to human curiosity. In 1824 a naval officer, Lieutenant Goldsmith set out to test the theory that 'a finger's weight can rock it, a man's strength cannot dislodge it.' He and a willing band of friends gathered at the stone near Porthcurno and managed to push it to the beach below. The frivolous officer was forced to pay the £130 8s 6d it cost to put the stone back in its resting place, a complicated and intricate operation involving a sturdy web of pulleys, ropes and beams.

'Log' is a Cornish verb meaning to move and this is just what the huge 66 ton rock does, though not so well since its untimely removal! I have not however, been tempted even to touch it having been enlightened about its powers over a quiet pint in a snug corner of The Logan Rock Inn. My informant suggested that a woman could become a witch by touching the stone nine times at midnight, and informed me that no criminal could make it rock; in both cases I would rather not put the claims to the test.

The Logan Stone now belongs to the National Trust. They acquired it, along with Pedn-vounder Beach and an Iron Age Promontory fort, in 1933 when the land was given to the charity by Sir Courtenay Vyvyan of Trelowarren, in whose family it had been held for eight centuries. One can't help but wonder what they would do if some heartless fool were to topple the great stone again. One hopes their flair for tackling tricky challenges would ensure it was again returned to its rightful throne.

A TOURIST ATTRACTION ... An early postcard depicts the Logan Rock with, one supposes, the photographer's assistant or a willing local man, perched atop the strange natural wonder.

GIANT'S STONE

TO MANY, Zennor is known for its Mermaid, but above the village is the seat of another legendary figure – the Giant of Carn Galver.

He was a gentle giant, protecting the people of Morvah and Zennor over whom he watched from a Logan Stone perched high above the villages.

Many Cornish giants are notorious for their evil natures, but the one time this giant killed a man he was stricken with grief. The fatal incident happened when he patted a young friend on the head in an affectionate gesture. His huge finger went straight through the poor man's skull. The sad story claims the Giant of Carn Galver never laughed again, his sorrow eventually bringing his life to an end when he died of a broken heart.

I chose this splendid photograph of the Giant's Stone taken in 1903 by Herbert Hughes, in preference to a modern shot because of the delightful characters in it.

Zennor, with its mermaid and giant, reminds us that Cornwall has been the breeding ground of some weird and wonderful tales. And the moorland inland retains deep secrets like some of the pools that lie across the landscape – the whole area has a revitalising quality. You cannot 'do' the moors of Cornwall – not even in a long life – because they are a renewing experience. There are always revelations in store.

GIANT'S STONE ... Another old photograph with what appear to be slightly unwilling subjects displaying the scale of the massive stone – the one a staid and Sunday-clothed pillar of respectability, the other, in less formal headgear, wedged uncomfortably in what may have been a giant's toehold in the rock.

THE TRISTAN STONE

THE TRISTAN legend is one of intrigue and jealousy – a powerful love story with all the sordid ingredients of a complicated romance involving a young couple and a rejected husband. The action is set in both Cornwall and Ireland, but it is in south-east Cornwall that you can find evidence to support the tragic tale.

Formerly known as the Long Stone, the Tristan Stone stands nearly three metres high on the roadside at Four Turnings just outside Fowey. This rugged pillar was originally erected near Castle Dore some two miles away, and the inscription on it suggests that it may well have marked the site of Tristan's eventual resting place. The words, running vertically down the stone, read 'DRVSTANVS HIC IACIT CVNOMORI FILIVS' – Drustanus lies here, son of Cunomorus. Scholars have identified Cunomorus as being King Mark of Cornwall whose son, Drustanus was Tristan.

Many people drive past this ancient pillar each day, but even though it no longer rests where Tristan's tomb is thought to be, it is definitely worth visiting the stone to admire and touch its rugged face and thought-provoking inscription which dates back to the sixth century AD.

CASTLE DORE

CASTLE Dore is a classic example of the earth reclaiming what man took to suit his needs. An Iron Age fort with two ramparts, the greater part of this once bustling defence has gradually eroded into the soil, unable to withstand the advances of the elements which march on regardless of time and history. It is not an obvious site and only the most determined visitor and Cornish resident is likely to discover Castle Dore, which lies to the north of Fowey on the road to Lostwithiel.

Excavations have revealed that the fort was built in 200 BC. But we must journey to the 6th century AD for one of the more fascinating moments in its military life. At this time it was occupied by royalty and the work on its defences, which were substantially remodelled, may well have been carried out by King Mark.

Tragic Tristram and Iseult are believed to have lived here, hence the weaving of Castle Dore into the complicated embroidery of information which makes the Arthurian legend so fascinating and so diverse.

I did not feel the atmosphere here that I did at Chun Castle, even though the fort was used as recently as the Civil War. Perhaps Mother Nature has worked especially hard to soothe the scars of war for a reason we, the modern visitor, cannot fathom, but battling ancestors would understand and welcome.

A novel called *Castle Dore* was a rare collaboration between two famous writers: one dead and the other then alive and well, living near here.

The novel is a retelling of one of the saddest love stories of all and

ANCIENT FORTRESS ... The outer defences at Castle Dore picked out in sunlight and shadow.

is set in the Cornwall of the nineteenth century. Back in the 1920s Sir Arthur Quiller-Couch, who lived at Fowey, set about writing a novel linking the Tristan and Iseult legend and Fowey, but he somehow tired of the idea and never completed the manuscript. It was only after his death that his daughter Foy reread the manuscript and in 1959 asked her friend Daphne du Maurier to complete it. After some hesitation, Dame Daphne did just that. In the words of Foy Quiller-Couch: 'Daphne did it so brilliantly, weaving her words into his, that I believe no reader will know where and when the shuttle was transferred from my father's hand into hers.'

AT WORK … Sir Arthur Quiller-Couch in his study on the eve of his 80th birthday, November 1943. An assortment of pens lies at hand, a Q paper-weight ready to hold down the completed manuscript should a Cornish breeze waft through the window.

WITHIN THE WALLS ... Today's quiet circle of greensward must long ago have rung to the sounds of warriors preparing for battle, from the Iron Age through to the Civil War.

CORNWALL

Here is my heritage,
Beyond the cliffs, the sea,
Here is my personal history,
Here is a part of me,

Here it is beaten in my mind,
Solid, firm and sure,
Beauty of my ancestors,
History pure, impure,

Come with me, explore my love,
My life, my land unwind,
Take a look at this Cornwall,
And the Celtic frame of mind.

Kirsty Gardiner

KIRSTY GARDINER, born 1971, lives at Tregony. She has been writing poems and illustrated stories from the age of eight. She loves drawing and painting. Kirsty has a strong Christian faith and is proud of her long Cornish heritage. She writes songs with her brother who is a pianist and scenic photographer, and helps her father in his local cleaning and maintenance business.

ROCKY VALLEY

ROCKY Valley sounds like the setting for a traditional Western with leather-skinned cowboys, war-crying Indians and dehydrated victims. Though canyon-like to look at, the similarities go no further. This lush green valley stretches to the Atlantic near Boscastle in North Cornwall.

It's a marvellously atmospheric place where the peace which surrounds you carries you back into the mists of Cornish history. We have to go back to the early Bronze Age to trace the origins of Rocky Valley's greatest treasures – the ancient maze-like carvings.

This early art work, reproduced here by Felicity Young, is relatively common in Britain but extremely rare in Cornwall. The purpose of the carvings is shrouded in mystery, though they are reminiscent of a sacred symbol among Hopi Indians and a religious emblem in India, all of which adds to the speculation about their creator and their age.

As you stand before these ancient carvings on a rock face behind the ruined mill just off the Tintagel road, it is interesting to ponder on what inspired the artist, and what, if any, links existed between North Cornwall and India at the time the carvings were produced.

Perhaps the clues and speculation lead the investigator on a false trail? We may never know, and maybe we would rather not discover the truth: Publisher Michael Williams says he heard of one investigator who persuaded a young woman to undergo hypnosis near the carvings. She went back in time and emerged from regression in a very distressed state, believing some form of human sacrifice had taken place.

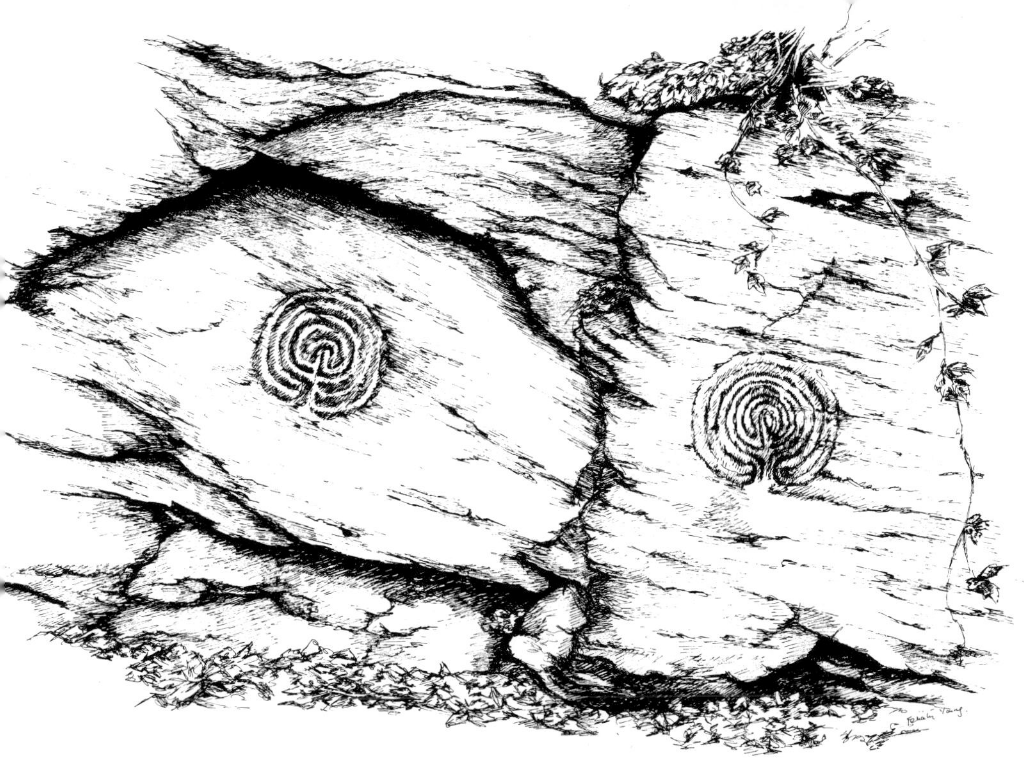

SYMBOLS FROM THE PAST ... These ancient carvings may never yield up their secret but the mysterious maze-like drawings will continue to fascinate all those who see them. Tintagel painter and book illustrator Felicity Young reproduces them here.

HAWKER'S CHURCHYARD

'A GOOD Sword and a trusty Hand!
A merry Heart and true!
King James his Men shall understand
What Cornish lads can do!'

SO WROTE Robert Stephen Hawker in his famous ballad *The Song of the Western Men*, a resounding tribute to the efforts of Bishop Trelawny which has withstood more than a century of musical fashions. The song, which still makes the hairs on the back of my neck stand up when sung by a group of Cornishmen, will remain a living epitaph to the Vicar of Morwenstow. But it must be said that there was a great deal more to Parson Hawker, as he was known, than Trelawny.

An unconventional and impulsive man, Hawker held strong beliefs on many matters, including the Christian burial of men who died at sea. He felt all mariners who fell victim to the fierce north Cornish coastline deserved the right to be laid to rest in consecrated ground, no matter what their religion or race. He resolutely recovered every body, even though it was often a gruesome task, and if you stroll into Morwenstow churchyard you will see the evidence.

The most obvious tribute to his devoted labours on behalf of the drowned is the proud and resolute figurehead of the *Caledonia*. She was a two hundred ton sailing ship from Arbroath which ran aground during a raging gale in 1842. Only one man survived the terrifying ordeal. Hawker made sure each and every one of his shipmates was brought from the sea's fatal clutches to the peaceful soil

by the stone church.

The churchyard has not been the figurehead's only resting place since the wreck of the *Caledonia*. In 1968 it was stolen, only to be recovered some weeks later from a field near Bideford in Devon. The reason for the theft is not clear, though one suggestion is that it was destined for the lucrative American antique market where it would no doubt have fetched a healthy amount! So who would take such a special monument? Joan Rendell, writing in the now out of print *Hawker Country*, says it probably was not local people because of the superstitions which surround it:

'It can now be revealed that what many local people hesitate to put into words, even when pressed, is that they believe that if one walks in an anti-clockwise direction around the figurehead thirteen times the spirits of the shipwrecked sailors will rise up and the figure will strike out with its sword!'

Hawker loved the peace and tranquility of his sheltered church and its hallowed grounds, but he also had another more secluded retreat tucked into the cliffs above the cruel coastline which claimed the lives of so many of his 'lost souls'. Hawker's Hut, which is owned by the National Trust, was built out of driftwood and provided a rustic sanctuary for the Vicar to withdraw to to write his poems, books and songs, and pen his letters and sermons. Here he would meditate, smoking his pipe of opium and reflecting on the Cornish scenes around him which so shaped his life. Many eminent authors have written of the Vicar of Morwenstow, I simply commend the Hut to you as an ideal place in which to rest and get to know the man for yourself.

REMOTE RETREAT ... Few churchmen can ever have had a sanctuary with such incredible views as Hawker must have enjoyed, here in his hut on the cliffs.

NEVIL NORTHEY BURNARD

THE CATHEDRAL of the Moor is a formidable tribute to the strength of rural worship in Cornwall. To be honest, it's not Altarnun Church itself that first catches your eye as you enter the moorland village, rather the 130 foot tower which took more than a devoted generation to construct. The building, in its unlikely setting, stands as a permanent reminder of the fervour of religious passion which stirred in the heart of the Cornish countryside, and both its exterior and interior are worth exploring.

Take time to examine the various stone monuments and you will no doubt stumble against two headstones signed by teenage genius, Nevil Northey Burnard. The son of a stonemason, he was born in Altarnun in 1818 and at an early age, using no more than nails sharpened on a grinding stone, he displayed an outstanding skill for carving. It was a talent which was to take him to London where he sculpted for the Prince of Wales and exhibited at the Royal Academy.

At the tender age of fourteen, Burnard carved two headstones: the first, to the west of the Isbells' tomb, is probably that of his grandparents and depicts an eagle flying into rays of sunlight. The other, by the vicarage gate, was his first effort, produced for a young cousin, and depicts the Angel of the Last Trump. Here, instead of engraving the letters, Burnard chiselled round them so each stood out in relief: a simple but extremely effective design.

Sadly this talented man, with an enviable gift that bought him the praise of society, died penniless and forgotten in Redruth Workhouse. A tragic end for an artist whose feel for stone was legendary.

STONE MEMORIAL … A memorial not only to the man who lies buried here but to the extraordinary talent of the 14-year-old Nevil Burnard who carved the headstone with such skill.

KING ARTHUR'S HALL

THE MYSTERY surrounding King Arthur is one that will probably never be solved. Too many people have joined the debate – both sides equally adamant about the myth or the reality of a man who has unwittingly helped, in modern times, to create a lucrative tourist trade.

One man who believes in King Arthur is author Colin Wilson. In *King Arthur Country in Cornwall*: 'Commonsense tells us that there is no smoke without fire. The other legendary king of romance is Charlemagne, and we know he existed, because he made his mark all over Europe, and there are hundreds of records. Arthur was an obscure British general who lived three hundred years before Charlemagne, in a remote corner of the then-known civilised world and there are no contemporary records, unless, as is likely the references in Nennius are quotations from such documents.

'But the spread of his fame, from Wales to England, then across Europe, suggests that he was a real person. In fact, I find it difficult to call to mind any famous mythical figure who was absolute and pure invention; even Dr Faustus really existed.'

I tend to favour the idea that if there were such a king, he was a hardened fighter, popular with the women and well travelled, and not a knight in shining armour astride a majestic grey stallion. The 'rough-diamond' image would fit better with the landscape with which he is linked, including the wild and windswept King Arthur's Downs where only the tough moorland ponies can withstand the elements for any length of time.

It is on these downs that you come across an archaeological puz-

Felicity Young.

MEDIAEVAL MYSTERY ... King Arthur's Hall was probably already ancient in the time of the traditional adventures of the Knights of King Arthur. The moorland of Rough Tor and Brown Willy, seen here through the haze, must, however, have looked much the same.

zle. The outline of King Arthur's Hall is made up of a number of stones which form an incomplete rectangle. Records of the earthwork date back to the sixteenth century, but the Hall has been a curiosity for many more years. Experts say it is either neolithic or mediaeval, and similar to sites found in Wales and Ireland.

Weathering of the banks around the enclosure has enhanced the visual impact of the stones which may give a false impression of the site and its past uses. Fortunately enough remains of the Hall to feed the imagination and no doubt every walker's mind paints a different picture of its past.

PORTRAIT … The haunting representation of Christ which hangs on the wall of a tiny Cornish Church.

ST VERONICA'S HANDKERCHIEF

TRUDGING around museums and stately homes as a child, always prompted me to search for the unexpected, a juvenile response to what I perceived as an 'adult' setting. Sometimes it was an unfulfilled hunt for a family ghost, other times a desperate attempt to discover something no-one had ever seen before.

I remember one occasion when I found a huge painting which covered a whole wall. As I walked up and down past it I realised the eyes of the men in the picture followed me. With tremendous excitement I babbled the strange news to my parents only to find it was a feature people travelled from all over the country to see!

Later though I was to witness another canvas phenomenon of arguably greater intrigue in the moorland village of Blisland. Hanging on the north wall of the splendidly named Church of St. Protus and St. Hyacinth, is a peculiar portrait of Christ wearing his crown of thorns. Under the framed reproduction lies an inscription which says it is 'of the celebrated painting by Gabriel Max, an Austrian born 1840.' The extraordinary feature of the artist's haunting interpretation of Jesus is that if you watch the eyes closely they suddenly open!

Once you have stood in front of the 'divine' face it is easy to understand why a television programme in 1981 which referred to the portrait by its unofficial title of 'St. Veronica's Handkerchief', stirred up an innocent, if misleading, belief that this was an even greater find than the Turin Shroud. It may only be a clever trick of the artist's brush, but it brings a special dimension to the atmosphere of the moorland church. I believe the original from which

AT PEACE ... Blisland Church and churchyard beneath a moody summer sky.

VILLAGE GREEN ... Blisland boasts the only village green in all Cornwall.

this reproduction is taken belongs to a private collection in Prague. One wonders how much it is worth in these days of million pound art deals.

The church itself, Norman in origin, is an intriguing mixture of the grand and the simple. As you enter through the solid wood doors, you are struck by the ornate splendour of the altars and their protective half screens, decorated in a rainbow of colours tinged with gold.

I chose to sit in the pew to my left as I entered, the patterned stone tiles beneath my feet. From here you can take in the high altar in all its glory, and the Cornish stone pillars, which list noticeably to the right.

A fellow traveller had written in the visitors' book: 'words cannot do justice to this church' – I quite agree!

DOZMARY POOL

THE RIDE to Dozmary provided me with an autumnal breath of fresh air, clearing the stale scents of town from my head. My heart lifted with every lively stride taken by my sturdy mount, and she seemed glad to be given the opportunity to hack across the wild open countryside. It was a morning dulled by the grey clouds that often linger over the moor.

The sights and sounds of this area are unique: a heron flapping lazily between the trees on the banks of the very young Fowey river, the distant call of a cow to her calf. This is the time to reflect on the wonder and beauty of wild Cornwall. I am privileged to live here – a land which still resists, to a certain extent, the dabbling hands of meddling developers.

Chateau Potensac is a Welsh cob x Arab, born and bred right here on the moor – this is her territory and she covers it effortlessly with her noble ears pricked. She belongs to Jane Talbot-Smith, Cornwall's first Master Saddler, who runs Blisland Harness Makers from her sheltered moorland cottage down in the Fowey valley. We rode together, talking of our shared passion for horses, Jane outlining the 'who's who' of the moor as we passed the land of assorted farmers.

Dozmary appeared at the end of the steep climb, rippling under the harsh strokes of a fresh wind. It lay before us, dark grey in colour, giving nothing away, yet calling us to look closer.

Jan Tregeagle was an evil man whose blatant disregard for other people's lives was bound ultimately to lead him to the harshest penalties. He murdered his first wife and children, then married a

STILL GLIDES THE STREAM ... The author reflects beside the narrow ribbon of water which grows eventually into the majestic Fowey River.

DOZMARY POOL ... Tamsin Thomas and Jane Talbot-Smith, and their mounts, pause after the stiff climb to the mysterious brooding water of Dozmary Pool. Neolithic and Bronze Age arrowheads and relics of even earlier man have been found along the margins of the pool and archaeologists think burnt peat and charcoal remains could indicate deliberate land clearance for the browsing animals.

line of heiresses, killing each for her money. He even chose to end his life of crime by selling his soul to the devil – a strange deal for a man who spent his years carrying out 'devilish' deeds! So what has all this got to do with Dozmary Pool? Shortly after his death, Tregeagle was summoned to Bodmin court as a witness in a trial involving an unpaid debt. The debtor denied all knowledge of the loan believing that Tregeagle, who was the only one to witness it, was safely underground.

Unfortunately for him the dead man's ghost made a startling appearance, terrifying the defendant who eventually employed a vicar to exorcise the wicked spirit. Tregeagle's ghostly form was banished to Dozmary Pool to empty the lake with a leaky limpet shell.

The story goes on, but it is the picture of the wicked Tregeagle labouring fruitlessly on top of Bodmin Moor which has stayed with me since I was a child. Any drive over the moor would involve lengthy pleas to my father to repeat, yet again, this strange and sinister story. It was only in later years that I was to discover the more romantic nature of this bleakly sited oasis.

It was the many moods of Dozmary that first attracted me to linger on its barren banks where the moor meets the water at seemingly the same level. I was not the first to detect the pool's distinctive atmosphere. Sir John Betjeman referred to 'a brooding melancholy, especially at evening' over Dozmary. I once picked my way along the stony path at the break of what promised to be a gorgeous Cornish Sunday. The pool was shrouded in a mist which provided a protective, translucent blanket over the mirror-like surface of the still water.

Standing alone in this mysterious world of natural peace I waited for a clenched fist to break from below the surface clutching King Arthur's bejewelled sword Excalibur, for it is said that this is the pool into which Sir Bedevere was ordered to throw the majestic weapon by the dying Arthur. A romantic story or the stark truth? I cannot answer these questions, nor would I seek to for fear of shattering delicious illusions, though I am tempted to one day try wading across the pool to test the theory that it is bottomless!

ROUGH TOR

I CLEARLY remember the struggle to reach the summit of Rough Tor. I lost my sense of humour half way up, my breath at the three-quarter mark and the use of my legs at the top. But don't let me put you off because the walk was worth every ache and moan when it reached its climax at 1296 feet. I stood, a proud observer, on my craggy balcony, the beautiful County of Cornwall resting at my feet: a crystal isle floating in a liquid blue sea.

Rough Tor, the second highest point in Cornwall after neighbouring Brown Willy, affords a view beyond description on a clear day, similar to that enjoyed from an aircraft flying below the clouds in the glint of the morning sun. I would imagine it loses some of its charm when climbed on a muggy day, the damp Cornish mist shrouding the view like a mourning veil.

There are those who speak of a ghost that walks the peak of Rough Tor, and there have been suggestions that sinister events have taken place here. I will not dwell on these tales as I have always found my visits to be a refreshing tonic, not least because of the peaceful quiet that surrounds you when you climb into the clouds.

Rough Tor, pronounced row, lies three miles south east of Camelford and was given to the National Trust in 1951 by Sir Richard Onslow, with the 43rd (Wessex) Division, as a memorial to its men who fell in the Second World War. The 174 acres of moorland cared for by the Trust includes a Bronze Age settlement site, hut circles and enclosed fields, some with lynchets, so there's plenty to see even if you decide you can't face the walk!

SUMMIT … Rough Tor's highest point – the moorland around was used by early man and yields a rich harvest for the archaeologist from Bronze and Iron Age remains to traces of mediaeval farmsteads. Below, *cattle still graze the slopes below Rough Tor.*

KING DONIERT'S STONE

WHEN KING Doniert drowned in 875 I wonder what impact it had on the Cornish community? There were no newspapers then to communicate the news immediately, no television cameras to capture the harrowing scenes of mourning. But he was the reigning King of Cornwall and the loss must have been great, even if the news took a while to filter through the county.

The memorial to this monarch who so tragically lost his life, stands to the side of the road which links Redgate and Minions. There are two stones on the site; one is tall with interlaced carving, the other is small and squat with a clear inscription which claims it is erected 'for the sake of King Doniert's soul'. He is often described as the last of the Cornish Kings, but this description is more likely to belong to King Ricatus who ruled Cornwall in the tenth century.

The stone is a fine memorial to King Doniert, having steadfastly fought the ravages of time, but it is sad that it pays tribute to a man who somehow drowned in an idyllic spot where the River Fowey now appears to be so tranquil and attractive.

SKETCHPAD IN HAND ... Felicity Young at work, photographed beside Charlotte Dymond's monument below Rough Tor. Charlotte was murdered at this spot by her jealous lover on a Sunday in 1844. Felicity, a watercolour painter, lives at Tintagel with her husband Ian, daughter Hazel and dog Arthur. Since 1984 she has contributed over two hundred illustrations for an extensive range of Bossiney titles. Recently she made her debut as a Bossiney author with Curiosities of Exmoor.

TRETHEVY QUOIT

WHEREAS Lanyon Quoit in West Cornwall gives the impression of having been constructed in a neat and almost precise fashion, Trethevy is noticeably more crude and bold in design. Its capstone, which is some four metres long, lies at a seemingly haphazard slant over the top of the rough stones which support it.

Despite its primitive look the quoit is a rare relic of the megalithic age being one of only two surviving quoits with a second burial chamber inside – the other is at Zennor.

Trethevy Quoit, which stands between Minions and St. Cleer near Liskeard, was probably erected 2000-1500 years before the birth of Christ, as a monument to an ancient dynasty of chieftains. Originally it would have been covered in earth to form a burial mound.

At its base is a small gap which leads into the heart of the quoit. I have to admit that I have never had the courage to venture inside, being fearful of what I might find or indeed meet! Some believe the gap is to allow the spirits of the dead to escape, others that it is where food could be passed in to sustain those interred through the journeys of death and some claim it is to stop the spirits escaping.

The other mystery at Trethevy is the small hole in the corner of the capstone through which you can stare at one small section of the sky, as if being directed to something in particular, a star perhaps? I have never been there at night to see. One idea put to me was that the hole might have been used during construction, but the question then is, how was the hole drilled? I leave this to you to ponder when you visit the quoit.

REMARKABLE STONES … This early postcard – the original in colour – is doubly interesting because on its reverse the writer confides the Cheesewring is near his own home. 'Quite a lot of people visit it,' he says.

THE CHEESEWRING

THE CHEESEWRING was indisputably once a witch's initiation rock and the top stone is still said to turn when it hears a cock crow! So says Britain's number one ghost hunter, Peter Underwood, in his book *Mysterious Places*. There is certainly an intriguing atmosphere about this puzzling formation which lies on the eastern side of Bodmin Moor. The first impression you get on visiting the site is that it must be man-made, but the general view is that it is a puzzling but natural, formation. The grey/blue stones – the smaller ones are at the bottom – seem to envelope you like a comforting suit of armour, welcoming you to the peaceful heart of this stone-clad arena where you can shelter from the ever present moorland breeze. Here you can rest from the bleak face of the moor and take stock of the varied treasures protected by the barren landscape which can at a moment's notice turn hostile and distinctly unwelcome.

Schizophrenic Bodmin Moor is not an easy place on which to live or farm, but just below the Cheesewring you will find the remains of Daniel Gumb's hut, one of the strangest homes in Cornwall. Born in the 1700s, he was clearly a gifted child, mastering the principles of algebra and Euclid at an early age and developing a fascination with astronomy. He lived in his cold stone home through three marriages, free from rent, taxes and the ignorant eyes of those who didn't understand his genius.

Daniel Gumb may have had a brilliant mind but he chose to live a simple life with his various wives, and children, all of whom he christened himself being a God-fearing man, if not a churchgoer.

Stone formed his home and his notebook – his chiselled diagrams still exist on the huge stone slab which formed the roof of his hut – and hostile as the cavern may appear at first glance, if you sit at its entrance and look out over the view before you, you can begin to understand why he found refuge in his little moorland home.

DANIEL GUMB'S CAVE … Opposite, the humble home of a mathematical genius. He earned his living as a stone mason but spent much of his time gazing at the stars and wrestling with mathematical problems. Above *– what seems to be a diagram demonstrating Pythagoras' theorem still remains for today's schoolchildren to wonder at.*

AGAINST THE SKY ... Almost impossible to believe this apparently delicately poised stone structure is a natural phenomenon.

A TIMELESS SCENE ... Livestock, unconcerned by the camera, browse contentedly on Cornish moorland.

THE HURLERS

THE MOORLAND village of Minions has a special place in my heart, not just because I have always loved walking the windswept landscape nearby, but because it is where I first started to really notice ancient mysteries. It is true that as a young child I had been taken to visit the famous sites like Stonehenge, but then my juvenile imagination had turned the massive pillars into nothing more than friendly giants or screens from which to hide from parents' prying eyes. It wasn't until my teenage years, when on a rock climbing expedition to the Cheesewring Quarry, that I first saw the Hurlers and started to wonder about these carefully preserved remnants of the dim and distant past. I have to admit that, at the time, I was dragging my feet behind the main party not altogether keen about the prospect of scrabbling my way up what appeared to be a sheer, smooth rockface, but my feelings of cowardly guilt were erased at a stroke as I walked into the middle of the stones that make up the Hurlers.

Similar to the legend surrounding the Merry Maidens Stone Circle, there is a story about the Hurlers which suggests they were once men who dared to play the old Cornish sport of hurling on a sacred day and were turned to stone for their sins. In fact the three interlocking rings which make up the Hurlers, were probably erected in the Bronze Age and, given the power that many say the stones convey, may well have had a religious or healing use.

I have not felt any physical power when visiting and touching the Hurlers, but am convinced that they must contain a tremendous force which has so far, protected them from more modern influ-

ences. Without such power how could they have withstood the effects of the mining industry which, at one stage, enjoyed huge success in the area? And is it not likely that the strength lying within the stones is also the barrier which somehow prevents them from being harmed by man who can now drive close to the site?

I leave you at the Hurlers, as I have been left before, with a task – to count the stones. I think, like me, that you will find the job impossible. But if you do succeed I must warn you that in the past there have been stories of people who have counted them correctly and, as a result, suffered a misfortune.

'All that is really known
of the ancient state of Britain
is contained in a few pages.'

Dr Johnson in 1778.

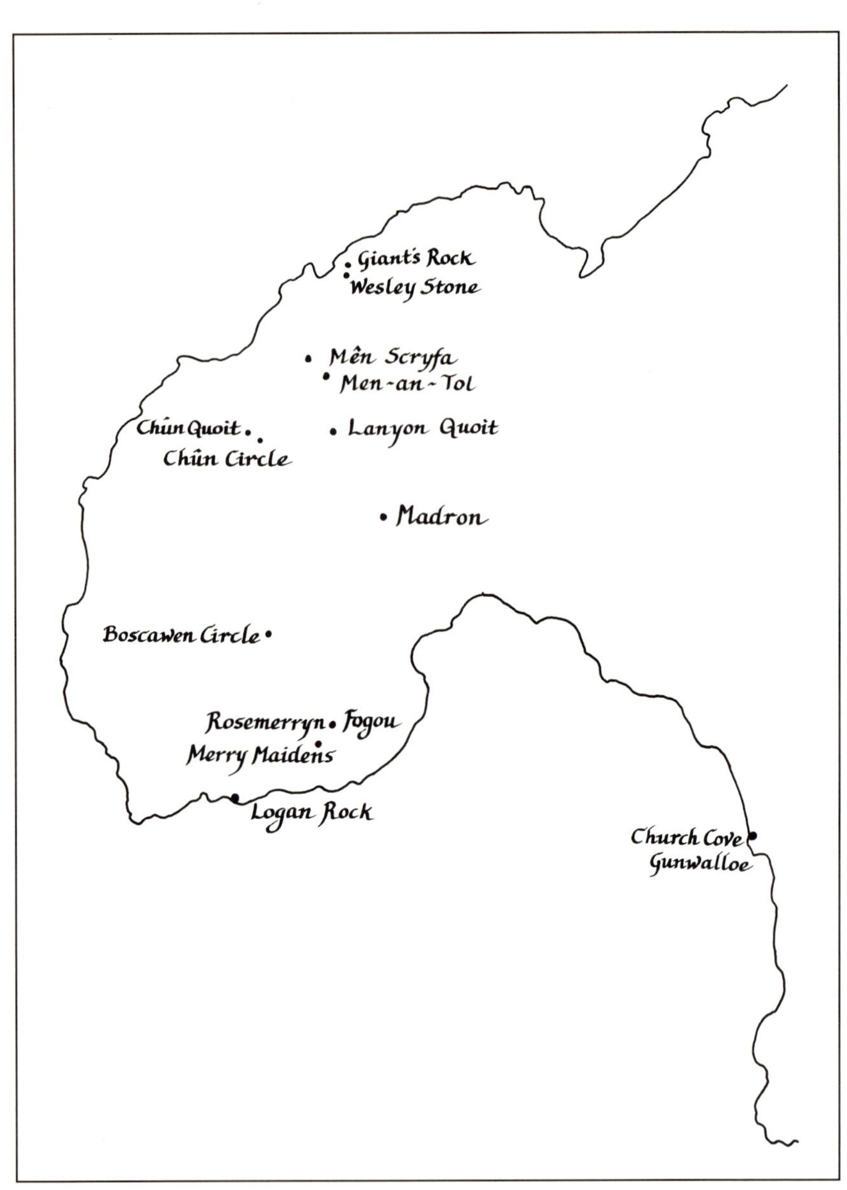

MYSTERIES IN THE

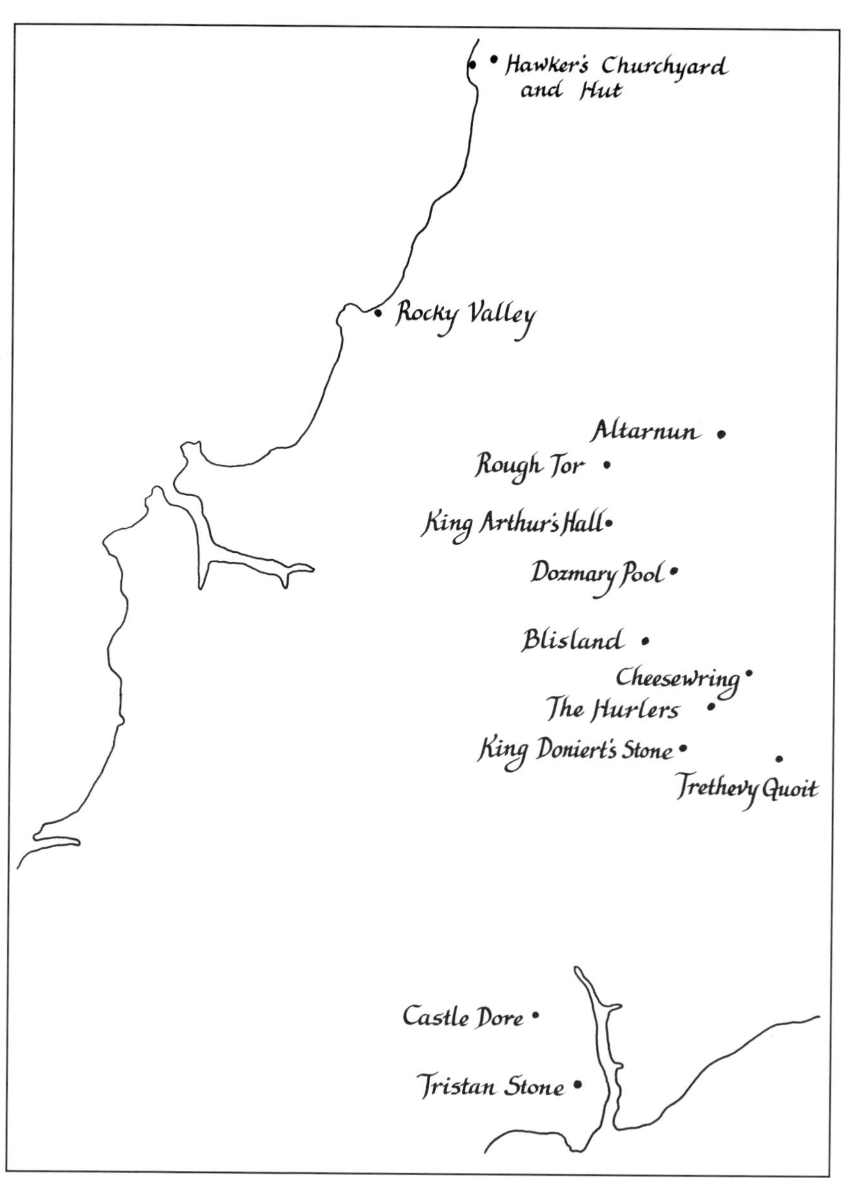

CORNISH LANDSCAPE

MORE BOSSINEY BOOKS ...

AROUND NEWLYN, MOUSEHOLE & PAUL

by Douglas Williams

In a skilful combination of research and interviews – and a rich harvest of old photographs – Douglas Williams shows the powerful spirit that draws people back to this corner of West Cornwall has not been quenched.

MOUNT'S BAY

by Douglas Williams

In words and pictures Douglas Williams takes us from Land's End to Lizard Light, the most westerly and southerly point of Cornwall, enclosing a bay 'as majestic as any in Europe.'

DAPHNE DU MAURIER COUNTRY

by Martyn Shallcross

A special look at Cornwall in which the internationally-famous novelist set important stories.

'A treasure chest for those who love Cornwall and the du Maurier novels.' Valerie Mitchell
The Packet Group of Newspapers

SUPERSTITION AND FOLKLORE

by Michael Williams

A survey of Westcountry Superstitions: interviews on the subject and some Cornish and Devon folklore.

'*... the strictures that we all ignore at our peril. To help us to keep out of trouble, Mr Williams has prepared a comprehensive list.*'

Frank Kempe, North Devon Journal-Herald

MY CORNWALL

A personal vision of Cornwall by eleven writers then living and working in the county: Daphne du Maurier, Ronald Duncan, James Turner, Angela du Maurier, Jack Clemo, Denys Val Baker, Colin Wilson, C.C. Vyvyan, Arthur Caddick, Michael Williams and Derek Tangye with reproductions of paintings by Margo Maeckelberghe.

'An ambitious collection of chapters.'

The Times, London

GREAT HOUSES OF CORNWALL

by Jean Stubbs

'*... explores seven National Trust properties, digging deeply into the history of the contrasting area of Cornwall.*'

John Marquis, The Packet Group of Newspapers

AROUND & ABOUT THE FAL

by David Mudd

'David Mudd's book brings to life the many aspects of one of Cornwall's most loved rivers.' Sarah Foot, Cornish Scene

SAINTS OF THE SOUTH WEST

by James Mildren

'This book, well illustrated with photos and sketches of buildings, monuments and the countryside associated with them, is a marvellous taster.'

Dr James Whetter, The Cornish Banner

E.V. THOMPSON'S WESTCOUNTRY

A memorable journey: combination of colour and black and white photography from Bristol to Land's End.

'*... the well-known novelist takes us on a memorable journey ... tells us of "the style and spirit of the region, its tone and tempo."*' Western Times and Gazette

COASTLINE OF CORNWALL

by Ken Duxbury

Ken Duxbury has spent thirty years sailing the seas of Cornwall, walking its clifftops, exploring its caves and beaches, using its harbours and creeks.

'*... has used his unique experience of sailing around Cornwall ...*' Cornish Scene

THE CRUEL CORNISH SEA

by David Mudd, 65 photographs

David Mudd selects more than 30 Cornish shipwrecks, spanning 400 years, in his fascinating account of seas and a coastline that each year claim their toll of human lives.

'This is an important book.'

Lord St Levan, The Cornish Times

CASTLES OF CORNWALL

by Mary and Hal Price, 78 photographs and map.

St Catherine's Castle and Castle Dore both at Fowey, Restormel near Lostwithiel, St Mawes, Pendennis at Falmouth, St Michael's Mount, Tintagel, Launceston amd Trematon near Saltash. Mary and Hal Price on this tour of Cornwall explore these nine castles.

'*... a lavishly illustrated narrative that is both historically sound and written in a compelling and vivid style that carries the reader along from one drama to the next.*'

Pamela Leeds, The Western Evening Herald

100 YEARS AROUND THE LIZARD

by Jean Stubbs. 150 old photographs.

A beautiful title, relating to a magical region of Cornwall, well illustrated, with text by the distinguished novelist living near Helston.

'*... writes with the skills of a professional novelist, the knowledge which comes from living here, and the enthusiasm which an enquiring mind can develop.*'

The Western Morning News

We shall be pleased to send you our catalogue giving full details of our growing list of titles for Devon, Cornwall, Dorset, Somerset and Wiltshire as well as forthcoming publications. If you have difficulty in obtaining our titles, write direct to Bossiney Books, Land's End, St Teath, Bodmin, Cornwall.